No Small Thing

No Small Thing

Gabriel Fried

Four Way Books
Tribeca

Library of Congress Cataloging-in-Publication Data

Names: Fried, Gabriel, 1974- author.
Title: No small thing : poems / Gabriel Fried.
Description: [New York] : Four Way Books, 2025.
Identifiers: LCCN 2024035151 (print) | LCCN 2024035152 (ebook) |
ISBN 9781961897342 (trade paperback) | ISBN 9781961897359 (ebook)
Subjects: LCGFT: Poetry.
Classification: LCC PS3606.R54 N6 2025 (print) | LCC PS3606.R54 (ebook) |
DDC 811/.6--dc23/eng/20240802
LC record available at https://lccn.loc.gov/2024035151
LC ebook record available at https://lccn.loc.gov/2024035152

This book is manufactured in the United States of America and printed on acid-free paper.

Four Way Books is a not-for-profit literary press. We are grateful for the assistance we receive from individual donors, public arts agencies, and private foundations including the New York State Council on the Arts, a state agency.

PROUD MEMBER

We are a proud member of the Community of Literary Magazines and Presses.

Contents

I. *Older Boys*

II. *Schoolyard Evangel*

III. *Stay, Illusion*

No Small Thing

I. *Older Boys*

HART

As a boy I pulled a wagon up a hill

As a girl I pulled a wagon up a hill

collecting timber for the things boys

collecting timber for the things girls

need it for: swords, dogs, rafts, kindling.

need it for: swords, dogs, looms, baskets.

I named the wagon Hart, my father's

The wagon was my heart, hauled behind

middle name. It was red as that deer,

my body. Its red was crusted red

the handle its antlers. This was back east,

with blooms of rust. This was back east,

3

closer to the city and the ocean

where mountains pinned the sky around us

than I knew; we had a little tractor,

like a groom; we had calluses,

a chainsaw, a tiller, other tools.

a chainsaw, three shovels, other tools.

*

As a boy I foraged blackcaps off the vine

As a girl I foraged blackcaps off the vine

and brought them home for mom to jam

and brought them home for mom to jam.

for me. My hands were bloodied

4

For me it was the first time each year

with their blood and my blood from where

                I'd bloody my hands that startled me;

thorns stuck me. My thumbs were swollen,

                by the time I picked berries, I couldn't

as if from pride, salt, or lust; my lips

                pretend their blood was blood or that my lust

were purple from the share I fed the boy

                to be a hero with a story could be so humdrum.

within myself, crushed against my tongue

                Sometimes I wonder what a memory

like lipstick in tubes at Oma's vanity.

of happiness means, though—that swollen thumb.

*

As I boy I spun in circles as a girl

As a girl I spun other children in circles,

transforming or a girl whose world transforms:

a pinwheel of arms carving its circumference

Diana Prince, Maria Rainer, Dorothy Gale.

in air like a blade on ice or a ritual fire.

The world around me streaked at light

Streak from me, my feather siblings;

speed, the never-ending blur of passing

I won't let go. I am limber and strong,

out from a blow to the head, of needing

shoulders like the jaguar's jaws

to rescue or be rescued. I was a girl deserving

there's no escaping the safety of,

of attention, sacrament hidden in the pyx

your scruff secure in the all-knowing mouth,

of the boy who earns her; she retrieves him.

your body attended to and sacred.

Poolside Superhero Triolet

for Jared

Each time we speak a hero's name we shift
mid-fight, new skills becoming our
predicament. We are dactylic
each time we speak the hero's name we shift
to: Nightcrawler, Shadowcat, Scarlet Witch.
We're lithe and girlish boys with airy powers
each time. We speak a hero's name. We shift
mid-dive, new skills becoming ours.

THE MOLE

It's no small thing
to loom above a soul
you aren't sure of
as a group of boys.

We've surrounded
the mole we found
belly-up on the blacktop—
star-nosed, sunstruck,
the lack of damp
and dark around it
denouncing whatever
it may have felt
of belonging.

It was stripped to begin
with, now draped in
nakedness, the shame
of a membership revoked,
that certain, seen absence,
the lava blush of blood.

What even is it? Some sort
of half-form, a pupa,

marsupial, or maggot?
A kind of creature
someone saves
or pokes with a stick.
Some of us have been
jabbed in the ribs with
thick fingers or humiliation
recently enough
to know that ache;

and some have never left
a thing alone, nothing
built or born too prized
or sacred to be unmade,
pried beyond function
or recognition.

The spring air stinks
with what could happen.
The squeal or squirt
we've learned to shoot for
elongating among us.

Who's to say what best
prepares us for the world
that we will one day
lumber through as
middle managers.
Is it really tender-
heartedness?
Or is it sidestepping
the surrounding violences,
redirecting them toward
the unarmored, whose
panicky perfume is
radiant around us,
a splotch of memory
staining the asphalt
where we pick teams,
decide which side
we fight for.

OLDER BOYS

I'm going off again with older boys
who slouch in memorable shoes and coats
into the thickening forest or cars,

depending on their age, their chosen toy.
It never changes. Like a paper boat
gone floating off again with older boys,

caught in their current, I appear buoyant,
but gasp for air as I laugh at their jokes.
Into the thickening forest, our cars

first handheld (Hot Wheels, Matchbox), overjoyed
at being undiscarded, safe as smoke.
I'm going off again with older boys,

the indifference I'm hoping to exploit
yet to undo me, a hole I float
above, a thickening forest: The cars

they shouldn't be driving, the country roads
careening us away from country bars.
I'm going off again with older boys
inside the sticky fortress of their cars.

HIV Triolet

We were thin for different reasons.
I was fourteen. It was 1989,
and I wore shit-kickers with cut-off jeans
that wore thin. (For different reasons,
neither of us dressed right for the season.)
I sat in his Wrangler one seedy time.
We were thin for different reasons:
I was fourteen; it was 1989.

The Pact

My grandfather read me a poem
without metaphors or difficulty.
The book that he read from
looked hard and heavy.

He proposed to me a pact:
we'd recite the poem from memory
as soon as he got back.

Help me. Please. I haven't learned it.
He returns from work each night
at six like clockwork.

FIRST FETISH

When the switch comes down
I stick my rump up.

MISCHIEF NIGHT

No damage done
is ever just a joke
or game; our toys
are never real:
we play with
fire pokers and
bellows, meat
grinders and turkey
basters, funnels,
ratchets, a thimble,
thread and needle.
A Ziploc bag, big
enough to hold
a human head—
the whip we hide
away until the children
are in bed.

SWEETS

Remember the autumn of razor blades
hidden in candied apples and peanut butter
cups? Those first bites of impossible alertness?

We knew then the lifelong risk of our addiction,
each discovery in a drawer or cupboard
carrying a chilling thrill—not to mention

what we found on park benches
and food-court trays, or, once, the seatback flap
of a flight to Akron. It could be a Narnian delight

or the tempting green of something
Never-Landian . . . or it could be spoonfuls
of *anything*: honey, syrup, jam, treacle—

whatever trips that neural switch and triggers
the haywire surge to brain from tongue.
And this isn't just the cane-lust of the young;

no gateway drug: it is our crystal clearing,
our dopamine, our strobe-lit stroke.
Stick me with it, darling. Be my sugar coat.

SENTENCE

What happens when
we learn of death
by burst appendix
is not quite like
the other deaths
we learn we can't
outrun at five-and-a-
half or six, not quite
like tidal waves
or meteorites, atomic
blasts or plane crashes,
volcanic eruptions,
lightning strikes or great
whites, no, this one comes
for us from in us, a secret
irritation gone awry,
a pearl-less oyster-organ
we are better off without
and should not need
to stay alive, more like
the things we learn
to dread at forty-four-
and-a-half or forty-five.

SCRAP

A paper torn and left apart, a deed
or baseball card ripped at the heart
in an age-old argument of boys
or sisters, of sparrows fighting
over discarded
crumbs.

Conjuration

Winter, snowbound, New England.
Natural to think of summer,
that plum other expanse when

we watched the children from the house—
a month since school let out,
since rules not worth breaking.

We thought their chants were random,
their arrangements haphazard,
forgetting nothing

is more dangerous than the games
of players who don't know
the rules or the stakes.

Now look. We age, we ache.

THE TIME WE BROKE INTO THE CHURCH TO PRAY

What had you given us? Just a compass,
a Swiss Army knife, a pack of wax lips.
How long did you think before we'd slip
into something you'd deem worse than mischief?

The church was just sitting there, a brick box
under a tree. Who knows what day it was?
(Not Sunday; we'd just hauled trash to the dump.)
And since no one in town bothers with locks

we waltzed right in as if we owned the place
and ran as fast as we could through the pews
(it just *seemed* like something we shouldn't do).
But that was our best version of disgrace

til someone (who?) suggested that we pray.
And nothing was the same, quite, after that.
Like we'd signed an indecipherable contract,
which some drunk dad had warned us of one day.

Poem

after Jenn Gihvan

I feel the poem but I do not write it down,
like the watercolor god at sundown,

the susurrus of opening the last jar of jam
from the last year my mother canned jam,

my silhouette on the bed in the stacks of books
I'd just brought home from the library, books

of poems I haven't read but already know
in my heart, fingertips, and nostrils, a knowing

that goes deeper, a future wellspring
still within the earth that will spring

in striking chorus after all when we emerge
from the ravages of this season, this spring.

BEFORE THE SERMON

New York City, ca. 1936

The big-top makes a chapel of the fetid
lot between the ballpark and the river,
where the air sticks like a rancid jam.

We wander in after the bout (the famous
one where Jews cheer on each blow
the German takes from the Black champ),
thinking maybe it's another brawl to scream at
with what's left of our throats—this one lawless,
bare-fisted, jabs like crowbars to the jaw
of anyone who's ever wronged us.
(We still have it in us, that thirst for
third-party blood, that fracas
of knuckles shattering in a cave of teeth.)

It is a girl up on the stage though, a girl
in white. Too young to be a nurse,
she's barely not a boy—hair short, flat
as a birch board—a girl who'd sell a good
cause at your door: mental hygiene, democracy
abroad, things even the hopeless hope for.

We live in cold-water flats, flophouses,
toolsheds. We are twenty, seventeen.

America is splashing cold water
on our faces, rubbing it under our arms
and in our crotches, our cocks
retreating like turtle heads, nipples
ruby sharp as we pull stiff shirts on,
heading out to hack at ice or hanging meat.

What kind of girl's a man of God?
one of us asks, as she begins. Some of us
leave then, the men who take a swig
of cold spring water expecting gin.

Immigrant Song

Thank you for the wilderness
you stole for me,
for the tenement built
near the factory
its furnace murmuring
Hold me Hold me Hold me

Wartime Triolet

We watch the war from far up on the hill.
We tremble at what's happening down there.
We're creatures who would not know how to kill.
We watch the war from far up on the hill
that used to seem as if it stood on stilts
above the earth. We breathed another air.
We watched the war. From far up on the hill,
we tumble toward what's happening down there.

The Majesty of Piero della Francesca

In Monterchi, in August, I lament not being pregnant,
      not because I can't afford to pay
the token fee to stand inside the cool, dark chamber

before Piero della Francesca's *Madonna del Parto*,
      but because the gesture of waiving
that fee for the pregnant (as the sign outside

describes) is one I yearn to have extended to me.
      Never mind that I'm a man,
an assimilated Jew, and (perhaps most disqualifying)

an American tourist. It is in the nature of witnessing
      Piero's work to crave inclusion,
even as it is almost inevitably withheld:

the two angels, mirroring each other at the tent-folds,
      could be completing an act of opening,
having spread the tent apart as the Madonna readies,

the graphic slit in her dress suggesting the imminence
      of a birth she seems poised
to perform herself—the long fingers of her right

hand already spreading the unfastened lips of fabric.
     For a moment before the illuminated fresco,
I am ecstatic at my improbable admission—

ecstatic that Piero's angels would anticipate, so
     many centuries in advance, the strength
of my agnostic hunger for transfiguration.

But then, creeping in, a doubt: to the Madonna's left,
     I can't help notice, one angel
(though, I'm told, an exact reflection of the other)

looks singularly ill from what suddenly it seems
     could only be my presence, his face sallow
with revulsion. And at that, even his twin, the picture

of heavenly health, seems indisputably at the brink
     of *closing* his half of the tent mouth,
whereas a beat before he seemed to stake

my entrance to the birth of God.
     But this is Piero's majesty:
not the withdrawal of an invitation never

actually extended, not exclusion from the sacred.
　　　Rather, in his perfect depthless field, rests
the static instant on which the impossible balances,

its flat, pregnant possibility infusing us. We, who
　　　otherwise might never know
the rapture of true communion, know it

in our unexpected longing. And if the curtain closes
　　　on my momentary grace,
it is not because I have been refused admission

to one viewing or another, but because
　　　I was granted transcendence for a spell,
momentarily forgetting the conventions of my body.

II.   *Schoolyard Evangel*

FLIER

Come to my sermon!
After school! By the swings!
Popsicles + Benedictions!
While supplies last!

Pilgrimage

I take you out beyond the fence
to where the dead dog dug a hole.
It's not yet dark or cold.
I say I've told our parents.

Above the branches, phone wires
give off an ancient hum.
Remember the noise last summer?
The cicadas were a bonfire

of sound we caught and dared
each other to eat alive.
I couldn't chew it when I tried.
It moved in my mouth like prayer,

and when I opened, it was gone—
vanished like sacrifice.
You said that I was lying,
that I spit it out or hid it with my tongue.

But a lie is something you can prove,
the blooming side of a dying tree.
We're here, I say from part of me.
You think I speak to you.

VISION

Another cobblestone Sunday—
they stream toward church,
greeted at the door by the preacher.

God's not there—I should tell them—
I saw him by the toolshed
when the nail came through my sneaker.

SCHOOLYARD EVANGEL

They say I have been sent. Who says?
Not my parents if that's what you're thinking.
Not my parents and not my pastor
neither. And not God. God's busy.

The other boys play contest games.
Some run like hares. Others huddle
like fat old toads. Both kinds please me,
how full they are of keeping score.

Sometimes one asks me what I'm doing
up here on top of the mountain
of old truck tires. I say I'm waiting.
For what? he asks. I tell him I

don't know but that when I do I'll tell
him so. The teachers must rely
on me the way they watch me watching.
Sometimes they stand in groups and look

my way together like a congregation
looks beneath the pulpit, or friends
on their backs guessing at
cloud shapes before a storm.

SCHOOLYARD BLESSING

Remember that the asphalt brings you joy
and asks for little
just a trickle
of blood

So much less than any other god
a spot of red
to brighten up
the blacktop

in exchange for all that joy
of stickball, double Dutch, and hopscotch
just a drop
you'll never miss
and never need

O skinned knee
Blessed be

Schoolyard Dirge

After rain, the blacktop is covered
with worms. Birds come, then sun

then my classmates with balls.
For the worms I sing a sad new hymn,

a low flat long dry song.

REVIVAL

Come inside my tent.
It is orange and can fit
standing up Uriah Lewis,
third tallest in fourth grade.

There is a canteen of Juicy Juice
blessed with stream water
the dogs lay down in,
and a Saltines tin of Triscuits.

For itches and sores, there is
Mercurochrome, Caladryl, a bag
of cotton balls. And a *Golden
Guide to Reptiles and Amphibians*.

Come inside my tent.
It is shady, the air is DEET-sweet
with secrets, ascending
like a cloud of repentance.

Bring your idols,
your action figures and trading cards,
the flags, the ire,
the magazines of the fathers.

Questions about an Atheist

What is the atheist nodding at so intently?
What does he think he understands?
What has happened since he seemed
satisfied with what he learned about whales
or mummies in social studies class?
Has he learned to spin a basketball on his finger?

Why does the atheist look so pleased by long division?
Why does he always show his work?
How does he make machine-gun sounds with his mouth
at recess and run so fast in his rainboots?
Who does he shout to after scoring goals,
his arm pointing to the sky?

Who gives the atheist permission to use matches
and sends him to burn up gypsy moth tents?
How does he know what sacrilege to report?
What surprises him in the darkened hallway?
Who crackles *Copy that* or *Ten-four*?

Confession of the Fourth-Grade Teacher of the Schoolyard Evangel

He looks at me like daddy would a lamb
on the farm: with affection but no mercy.
It's eerie. He's only nine-and-a-half.
When he was born, his sister was in my class…

I hear he's always been this way. The first-
grade teacher, Ms. Corn, got the alphabet
wrong one time. He just kept staring at her
with that *sense*. His gaze is disconcerting.

It's not that I think that he means me harm.
In fact, I've never heard a cruel word
from him. But can't intensity just hurt
sometimes? Like when the sun reflects off snow

on the drive to school, early, on a Monday.
You have to overlook a certain burn—
push through to what's ahead—to the turn
on Route 14 where there's nothing that can

save you: if a car's stopped up there, a deer,
you're done for. I mean *I* am. There's no way
through except the faith your hands will stay
true and the road, like always, will be clear.

Unrhymed Sonnet by the Atheist Grandfather of the Schoolyard Evangel

Look at that goddamn boy out in the field,
a goddamn evangelical in love
with his goddamn fancy. His parents named
him Gabriel, so what do you expect
but a child who thinks he's the herald
of transparent impossibilities.
I'll admit that he's a charmer, always
asking after work and family friends.
And there's a game we played on walks: he'd stomp
the pavement, which I'd tell him makes potholes
or turns stoplights green or red. I wonder
if he got a strange idea about himself
from that. Now I worry he'll start the wrong
goddamn war. Or stop the right one.

TESTIMONY

Our son has somehow hauled
the Olivetti typewriter six feet sky-
ward atop the upside-down

apple crate the migrant workers left.
Now he's clack-clacking
away up there on what

he's calling testimony.
Where he even learned that word
I couldn't tell you.

He's never been to church
and no one that we know has
ever been to church unless you

count the wedding of the widow
of the teacher who died
in the crash on the post road—

and even those he knows
who say they sometimes
think of church would never go

to one with testimonies:
the would-be Quakers
or Yellow Dog Episcopals.

Is he one of those about whom
they will ask one day: *What
is his story? How did he emerge*

from there or *them?* Like the duckling
raised by wolves, the stockbroker
pulled from the loins of

the Communist? What has he heard
out there in the world? What has
our neglect led him to discover?

Manifest

The people descend to the house of worship
        in a stream of congregation.

They are among the lucky ones: they have found a room
        that keeps their separateness together.

Across the river, in the city where the village used to be,
        an arena is half-full

of hope: a young starting pitcher has almost gone
        the distance.

Hasn't this happened before? That time
        we thought we'd cast a spell

until we discovered the baby in the corner
        unplugging lamps from the outlets?

Or the time we finally reached the western edge
        of the continent, standing atop

the cliff before a different sort of ocean, when

        all we could think to do was turn around,

retrace our steps, in search of what we must have missed?

Progeny

If you join the crowd that streams like salmon
toward the entry, perpetually
bursting through the narthex of the church

and into the sanctuary,
what you'll find above the backs and backs
of heads you'd recognize eventually

is the incongruous person
of your own child
from the waist up, as if levitating

over the congregation with a power
you admire as much as you fear
you'll come to question or covet.

Parenting Triolet

The little god has grown, a little god
no longer. Will he answer our prayers
now that he's lifted from our fog
a little? God, he's grown. A little god,
a little storm. A wolf among our dogs.
Something we hunt or run from—up the stairs.
The little god has grown, alit, dislodged.
No longer will he answer our prayers.

Prayer Triolet

A prayer insists on forming in my mouth.
Here it is, a hatching or exhaustion
of devotion. It is a birth or shout
the prayer insists on, forming in my mouth
as if another tongue, as if a spouse,
as if a spring. As if a storm's nausea
insists on frothing in my mouth:
here. It is a hatchling of exhaustion.

The Pastor

Who is the pastor fishing with in the river?
From up here on my rock I can see them casting,
water thigh high. I know they're speaking
from their shoulders and dog-tilt of their heads.
But their backs are to me; I hear nothing of their voices.

Once I saw the pastor with the butcher in waders
and his apron, blood-covered in the front.
Another time it was the county clerk.
And once the bishop! The pastor taught him a new knot.

But I don't recognize this person, who is barely
even shaped like a man and is dressed in trousers
green as sherbet. Doesn't he know those will scare the trout?

The pastor is a godly man—men who fish usually are.
Still, he's a man. I watch him in case some part's rotten.

If I Die Before I Wake,

will I still wake, startled by the silent
air above a room I cannot move in,
nothing like the silent hill
covered in snow before sleds,
or the tiny, indomitable roar
spring peepers made at night
when I was young?

Finally, will no one say *you mean small*
when I say *when I was young*?

SACRIFICE

The theologian explains God
Never asks Abraham to kill his son,
That God demands an *offering*
And not a sacrifice, one
He knows he'll refuse;
And, lo, Abraham complies
Because he has no doubt
That binding his boy and holding
A blade to his amber skin
Will never let his blood.

Well. I've never known a man
Who takes a child up a mountain
Without thinking for a moment
That he might come down alone.
And though I've never known
A god, I've been a boy, not so long
Ago. And I've been bound
At an altar and held to a knife.

III.   *Stay, Illusion*

Lucie Brock-Broido
1956–2018

WHENCE

Little-known zip code—
High cheekbones, mossy shoulders:
Monongahela.

HAGIOGRAPHY

It is tempting to make mothers out of art these days.
We've left the Rust Belt; it's art that mothers us.
With no one to tell us our birth stories,
we invent them. For instance, I was born in a painting
of a tent. From inside I saw a triquetra of the world
through the ripples of parted canvas. In the distance,
the chimney smoke of Lebanon, Pennsylvania.
Closer, the tallow-scented light, the right wing
of an angel of the antepenultimate order.
I emerged immaculate and high-collared
as a frescoed duke, a Jewess at communion
before a ragged congregation of miners.
Within the caravansary, I greeted every weary
traveler with a nod and gift: a minute horse encased
by a clear rubber ball, for instance. It was the Age of Embroidery,
the horse's saddle stitched with the tartan
of my stepsister's clan, an ancient band
of highway robbers stealing the King's English
to mete among the milliners, mutes, and foremen.
You see how this story goes? Is it not exactly as I told you?
Italianate and poorly framed, the painting I am born in
hangs in a diner by the jukebox, waiting for an urchin

to start the hymnal with a quarter. Although I am no patron
saint, no tomboy; I am no son of god. God is a verb
in this painting. Use it wisely and wildly.

A Hunger

You're forgiven for mistaking
for appetite the rumble
of trucks or the clank
of mechanical digging
on farms in the valley.
It is early evening
in truffle season,
zucchini engorge the garden.
The baby boar we found and raised
with love is hung with meat.
On cutting boards everywhere,
garlic, scallions, rosemary, and mint.

Tomorrow will be five days
since eating, five full days
since apricot and crust
of bread. The elders have all come
to me, experts in psychology,
neurons, physical education.
You're a boy, a growing boy!
they wail, *You'll waste away,*
your organs will devour themselves
like in a fairy tale! Eventually,
though, they wander off.

Other children need them:
a girl who never bleeds,
one who never stops;
a boy whose tear ducts
make no tears.

Now it's dusk. Lights flick on
in the village, stars like pinpricks
overhead. What do you think
powers them when God
has business? Within me
an engine whose fuel is wanting.
Can you hear it? It's what you take
for distant pangs of thunder,
a storm you think is coming
in the night.

ORIGIN STORY

I will stagger from the forest, a boy
transformed into a different boy,
dragging his leg like a story he's heard
of woundedness. When they see me, they will
drop their tools (their chalk and their jackhammers)
and rush to me, all of them at once now more
than men: champions and protectors.
They'll want to know everything, want to tell
their wives they asked the right questions.
Who am I? Where do I come from? What has—
what is the word—*befallen me?* I'll tell them
nothing of the nothing there is to tell;
that is no longer my biography,
and a silent child is also wise.
But after twenty-seven minutes I'll reveal
the one true lie about myself I know.
Then they'll take me to the stables for fitting.

Hansel's Children

Our father hunts us like a goblin.
Jubilant, we run where he can't follow,
squeezing in a coppice of cinnamon trees
or between the woodpile and our cottage.
He stomps his feet and shouts he'll burn
us out and chop us up for fricassee.
He says it will take all of us to make
a meal for him; he's right. We've heard him
creeping past us to the larder in the night.

ONE IS

not a lot of bottles;
a lot of punctured tires

not a lot of swarming hornets;
a lot of anaphylaxis

not a lot of pills;
a lot of years to kill

not a lot of choices;
a lot of self-loathing

not a lot of toes;
a lot of explosions

not a lot of words;
a lot of life sentences

not a lot of buses home;
a lot of blizzards

not a lot of hopes;
a lot of hope.

Ancestral Caution with Inadvertent Grammatical Substitutions

—after Aunt Johana "Honey" Altman (1892–1982)

Once along a time I was young like you.
Back then we had a different state in mind.

Children were children for longer,
but grownups quick. It was all then nothing.

One day, *Ausgelassenheit*, the next, the same
man next to you each night,

his smell enough to knock your socks up.
And then you were with child

or without child, having been a child
just last week, playing with the rabbits

you must slaughter, skin, and stew. Now
instead of reading tales of hidden girls

who sweep and sing, you are sick
from your own voice, sick from home

and dust. You achoo like the storm.
But the real storm comes later, and listen,

Liebchen, you would not believe
the nowhere it comes from—like gossip,

to begin, a thing you're sure means
something else, a mutter from under the road.

By the time you see you should have
joined the friends who fled, the words

are all over the wall. Out of a sudden
there are boots on the door.

"Man's Emotional Support Marmoset Disrupts Las Vegas Flight"

—Travel & Leisure

I was a Buffy-tufted child,
fourteen centimeters high,
southernmost explorer of my kind
in the forests outside Saquarema.
   I perched atop the fronds
of the tallest jelly palm,
refusing to bury my snout in sap
like some moral in a colonial story.
My auricular quiffs were handsome
as they sound, blown back,
filmic, by the airstream
skimming off the Atlantic.
   May I say *hematopoietic chimera*
now? It's what the sonneteers
are waiting for. (See their pencils
already floreting like balsa trees
in a storm.) My cells
are congenial; my marrow
could save you, second cousin
thrice removed. Let me stay here,
snug & private as a pocket
watch, far above the driest
forests beneath us. No one
will notice; I promise to be

as silent as a Pampas fawn
or the girl asleep in 17A,
ringlets like soursop petals
pressed against the glass.
I promise to do what
the overheard, overhead
voices ask.

CREATIVE NONFICTION

Here in the moment
of interpolation
(the god climbing in
to the animal's skin)
I claim my stake.

Introduction to Poetry

Your life has made a shadow on the wall.
That shadow is a poem, not your life.
Mistaking your poem for your life
might be your poem in your poem;
shadows sometimes look like living
things: a bird eating a spider, for example.
But your life is not the poem. It's the lie
described in the poem, according to a German.

The shadow makes a sculpture into song,
ringing like a sheet of dented tin, each strike
a preordained sound no matter how
you slant the hammer:
a lamb a lamb a lamb a lamb
Iamb Iamb Iamb Iamb

Correspondence from Madam Rachel, Purveyor of Eternal Youth, to Mister Walter Potter, Anthropomorphic Dioramist

ca. 1880

Most Splendid Immortalist: Herewith you have a letter sent
by my solicitor, written in my final leapt year, my sliver of pound cake—
the one meant to even off *everything*.

I have chosen my undergarments for the first epoch of bloodlessness:
the whalebone crinoline will reach you shortly. (I would never
eat a creature but am eager to be lowered indefinitely *in*.) The rest
of my costume I leave to your discretion; I have seen the perfection

of your kitten-wedding, the toms in their breeks, the kates in their
    mantuas—
though I trust you'll leave the Aquitaine hunting cloak for the feast of
    St. Hubert.
I find I am concerned more so with *pose*: how should I *be* in perpetuity?
What everlasting gesture of impulsiveness, epiphany, or wonderment?

And to remain unwrinkled, must I be upright? If so, I fear the chopines
impractical with no servants to support me; opera slippers, then,
    with tights.

Meanwhile, a final posthumous concern from my divan of ice:
what word will you use? It shan't be stuffed! Perhaps you will inspire one:
it can be your *Leotard*, *Hazard*, or *Shrapnel*,

your namesake's transliteration to *Cyrillic*. O! I'll be the eponym
of any stasis you decree, in whatever circus or garden party. Until then

I remain hopeful, however stiffly phrased and awkward, that you'll agree
to my request—to Taxiderm Me.

SON OF OUR LORD

Like the one who followed through
on the suicide pact,
enacted on a descending
count of three, I find myself
negative-numbered, phantasmagoric
in a fogged-up looking glass.

Cold Calls

Nothing miraculous happens
at the solstice. Dark at three

the day before and dark at three
the day after, a whip of wind

always on the verge of shattering
the pane, of letting in the men

who lurk perpetually outside.
They are campaigning for offices

their mother told them
they'd be perfect for: *You*

can do anything you want, she said.
Who wouldn't love that face?

The Vicar & the Vixen

I came upon a story called "The Vicar & the Vixen."
How strange

I can't remember when, whether from a book
or murmured

by a stranger out of nowhere at my ear, the woodlands
lipless

at dusk
in the heightening snow.

Persona Poem

Sometimes their eyes
betray us—the self
peering from behind
the portrait. Of all
the pornographies,
this one's my favorite.

Acknowledgments

Thanks to the following publications and their editors for previously publishing a number of these poems, some in earlier versions:

American Poetry Review, *Bennington Review*, *Great River Review*, *New Orleans Review*, and *Tin House*.

"The Majesty of Piero della Francesca" appeared in *Feathers from the Angel's Wing: Poems Inspired by the Paintings of Piero della Francesca*," edited by Dana Prescott.

"Schoolyard Blessing" was adapted for mezzo-soprano and violin by Carolina Heredia and premiered at the University of Missouri, Columbia in 2017.

Portions of this book were written during residencies at MacDowell and the Civitella Ranieri Foundation. I am grateful for the support of these wonderful organizations.

I am grateful, too, for a Research Council Grant from the University of Missouri System, which permitted me to spend the 2019–20 academic year focused on writing poetry, as well as to the College of Arts & Science and the Department of English at the University of Missouri for supporting my leave year.

My thanks to Four Way Books for continuing to support my writing and publishing it so well.

For their warmth and support, sometimes in ways they might not even have registered, thanks to Matt Farmer and Sarah Scheckter; David Degnan; Hannah Kauffman, Alyssa Ripley, and Annie Roustio; Molly McCully Brown; Molly Housh Gordon; Kerrin McCadden; Jessica Starr; and Micaela Bombard and Cass Donish.

Thanks to Alex Socarides, who has been reading my poems for more than a quarter-century, and to my growing-up family—my parents and siblings.

Thanks to Becca Hayes, my Co-Star business goose—partner in writing, not-writing, griping, guffawing, and deep sighing.

Forever thanks to Archer Fried-Socarides and Nate Fried-Socarides for so many things, including memorizing a new poem daily during those first, long pandemic months at home together.

Finally, something more than thanks to my beloved Martha McCrummen, Caitlin Gorman, and Fraser Kelly, without whom this book would not be. These poems are about various people, but they are all for her.

ABOUT THE AUTHOR

Gabriel Fried is the author of three collections of poetry: *No Small Thing, The Children Are Reading*, and *Making the New Lamb Take*. He is the longtime poetry editor for Persea Books and Director of Creative Writing and Associate Professor of English at the University of Missouri.

We are also grateful to those individuals who participated in our Build a Book Program. They are:

Anonymous (14), Robert Abrams, Debra Allbery, Nancy Allen, Michael Ansara, Kathy Aponick, Jean Ball, Sally Ball, Jill Bialosky, Sophie Cabot Black, Laurel Blossom, Tommye Blount, Karen and David Blumenthal, Jonathan Blunk, Lee Briccetti, Jane Martha Brox, Mary Lou Buschi, Anthony Cappo, Carla and Steven Carlson, Robin Rosen Chang, Liza Charlesworth, Peter Coyote, Elinor Cramer, Kwame Dawes, Michael Anna de Armas, Brian Komei Dempster, Renko and Stuart Dempster, Matthew DeNichilo, Rosalynde Vas Dias, Patrick Donnelly, Charles R. Douthat, Lynn Emanuel, Blas Falconer, Laura Fjeld, Carolyn Forché, Helen Fremont and Donna Thagard, Debra Gitterman, Dorothy Tapper Goldman, Alison Granucci, Elizabeth T. Gray Jr., Naomi Guttman and Jonathan Mead, Jeffrey Harrison, KT Herr, Carlie Hoffman, Melissa Hotchkiss, Thomas and Autumn Howard, Catherine Hoyser, Elizabeth Jackson, Linda Susan Jackson, Jessica Jacobs, Deborah Jonas-Walsh, Jennifer Just, Voki Kalfayan, Maeve Kinkead, Victoria Korth, David Lee and Jamila Trindle, Rodney Terich Leonard, Howard Levy, Owen Lewis and Susan Ennis, Eve Linn, Matthew Lippman, Ralph and Mary Ann Lowen, Maja Lukic, Neal Lulofs, Anthony Lyons, Ricardo Alberto Maldonado, Trish Marshall, Donna Masini, Deborah McAlister, Carol Moldaw, Michael and Nancy Murphy, Kimberly Nunes, Matthew Olzmann and Vievee Francis, Veronica Patterson, Patrick Phillips, Robert Pinsky, Megan Pinto, Kevin Prufer, Anna Duke Reach, Paula Rhodes, Yoana Setzer, James Shalek, Soraya Shalforoosh, Peggy Shinner, Joan Silber, Jane Simon, Debra Spark, Donna Spruijt-Metz, Arlene Stang, Page Hill Starzinger, Catherine Stearns, Yerra Sugarman, Arthur Sze, Laurence Tancredi, Marjorie and Lew Tesser, Peter Turchi, Connie Voisine, Susan Walton, Martha Webster and Robert Fuentes, Calvin Wei, Allison Benis White, Lauren Yaffe, and Rolf Yngve.